IT'S TOO HARD
TO BE
Saved!

WHO ARE YOU LISTENING TO?

DR. WANDA E. HUDSON

i

It's too hard to be saved!

Who are you listening to?

Wanda Hudson, D. Div.

Printed in the United States of America

First Printing, 2021

ISBN 978-0-578-89032-6

Becoming Wanda Publishing
P.O. Box 671
Union City, GA 30291

www.becomingwanda.org

Dedication

To all Believers willing to build a foundation based on the
TRUTH

Acknowledgments

First and foremost, I would like to give honor and thanks to God. Without Him none of this would be possible—with Him ALL things are possible.

I would like to thank my pastors, Creflo A. and Taffi L. Dollar, for continually teaching God's Word with simplicity and understanding. You have definitely made a mark that cannot be erased.

Thank you, *Collectives*: Dr. Angela Kinnel, Angelette Verdena King, and Carmelia Rankins for keeping me accountable in all things.

I am also very thankful for: Dr. Robyn L. Norwood, you made me come out of my comfortable place and made this process worthwhile—even at 8 p.m. and Dr. Deborah Isom, your teaching equipped and empowered me to accomplish this and so much more.

I would also like to thank those who took the time to answer the question "What does being born again mean to you?"

To my Parents: Jerome K. Carter, thank you for being the best dad a girl could ever have, and my mom, Barbara M. Carter—not a day goes by that I don't miss you and think of you. I know we'll meet again. Until then, Rest in Heaven!

To my Children and my Children's Children: thank you for always encouraging and supporting me. You bring me Joy!

Last, but far from least: I want to thank my husband, the love of my life, Dr. Roger C. Hudson. You have shown me what it is like to be covered and protected both spiritually and in the natural. Your love has always been unconditional-just like the Father's. Thank you for allowing God's love for me to be shown through you, until I could see it for myself.

Contents

Preface

"The meaning of being born again is spiritual renewal as a result of believing in and accepting Jesus Christ as your Lord and Savior." Angela, 46

When I am in my car, I usually listen to gospel music on YouTube. There's far too much talking and too many commercials on the radio. This particular day, I turned on the radio and of course the personality was "talking," but this time he said he had a young lady on the line who told him she received God as her Lord and Savior, but she couldn't live the life, or it was too hard to live the Christian life because she was not perfect. The radio personality wanted to know what the listeners thought.

At that moment God asked me, "What would you say to her?"

Instantly I answered, "I would say to her, Sweetie, none of us are perfect, but God is perfecting us. When you accept Him as your Lord and Savior, the Holy Spirit immediately becomes a part of you and He is going to help you be better—not perfect, but better, if you allow Him to. But this is a process!

Don't strive for perfection. Your goal should be a relationship with God. Don't compare yourself to other people in church who may "seem" perfect to you. God doesn't want you to be like anyone. He already knows who you are, and He wants to use you, not who you think you should be.

Get a Bible that you understand and read the Word for yourself. Find your brook—a church where the man or woman of God is teaching the Word, not just giving their opinion or playing on your emotions. Keep in mind that this may not be your family church; Big Momma may not even approve. Most importantly, don't let people or your feelings dissuade you. You have already taken the first step to an everlasting life, so keep moving.

God doesn't want you to wait until you get to heaven to enjoy the good life. He wants the best for you right now. Right here! It's all about renewing your mind and that means getting rid of the thought that you have to be perfect."

Then God told me, "That is what I want you to write about."

So here it is.

In writing this book, my hope is that new believers, and current believers who are at a standstill, will use it to build a foundation based on what the Word of God actually says, and not merely follow what they heard someone say. I want readers to know the truth, not tradition.

When reading this book, I want readers to understand they are not alone in their thoughts of obtaining perfection before being worthy to come to God. He already knows who you are, and He accepts you just the way you are.

Lastly, I want readers to know that it is NOT too hard to be saved.

So, congratulations! By accepting Jesus as your Lord and Savior you have taken the first step to having eternal life. The good part is you can have heaven right here on earth because your salvation has been purchased and paid in full by the Blood of Jesus.

"Being born again to me is not about being perfect! It is more about trying to live as Jesus did, knowing that you may fall short, but with faith and your belief in Jesus Christ you keep striving to live according to the Word." Brenda, 56

Chapter 1

Paid in Full

Your Salvation has been purchased by the Blood of Jesus

"From the Christian perspective, being born again means that you accept Christ in your heart and your slate is wiped clean. You basically start your life again in Christ. It's the same as renewing wedding vows, except you renew yourself in the Lord." Tiffany, 33

The Blood of Jesus Has Been Praised through Songs

"What can wash away my sins? Nothing but the Blood of Jesus. What can make me whole again? Nothing but the Blood of Jesus.[1]"

"The blood that gives me strength from day to day, it will never lose its power. It reaches to the highest mountain and it flows to the lowest valley. The Blood that gives me strength from day to day, it will never lose its power.[2]"

Just a couple of lines from these two songs proclaim the sentiment that the blood of Jesus is cleansing, it is comforting, and it is powerful. It is powerful enough to purchase your salvation so that there is nothing else you must do except receive it.

In Matthew, Jesus said, "for this is My blood and the [new and better] covenant which [ratifies the agreement and] is being poured out for many [as a substitutionary] for the forgiveness of sins Mathew 26:28, AMP. The New Living Translation states, "for this is my blood, which con

---

[1]   Nothing but the Blood of Jesus, written by Robert Lowry, 1876

[2]   **"The Blood Will Never Lose Its Power Lyrics,"** Accessed April 8, 2021. https//www.lyrics.com/lyric/7734887/Andre%C3%A9+Crouch.

firms the covenant between God and His people. It is poured out as a sacrifice to forgive the sins of many." In this scripture Jesus is prophesying (saying what is going to happen in the future). He is letting His disciples know that His blood would be a "signature" to the contract (covenant) that God has made to the believer. He is talking about you!

The Blood of Jesus is Symbolic

Blood has always been symbolic in the Old Testament. In Exodus, the blood of the Lamb was used as a symbol of protection. When God passed through Egypt He passed over the houses that had blood over and on the sides of the door, saving the Israelites from the curse that He placed on Egypt: to kill the firstborn male of every household (Exodus 12:7-13). The blood of animals has also been used as atonement (payment for a wrong) for sins (Leviticus 17:3-11). Unfortunately, these blood sacrifices had to be repeated since animal blood did not have the power to take away sin; it only had the power to cover or atone for sin. BUT the great news is that Jesus' blood has taken away our sin once and for all time!

I asked other believers what they thought when they heard the phrase "the blood of Jesus." Even though comments varied, going from a few words to an entire sermon, the common denominator is that the blood: redeems from sin, is perfect and makes people perfect (in God's sight), pays the price for our downfall, is powerful and delivers.

The blood is all of this and so much more. It Ratifies. It

is Redemptive. It is Cleansing. It Heals. It is Powerful and gives born-again believers Victory in every area of their lives.

The Blood of Jesus Ratifies

With the shedding of Jesus' blood, all believers, whether they be Jews or Gentiles (non-Jewish people), have the same rights and protection under the New Covenant (Ephesians 2:11-13), which only the Israelites originally had under the Old Covenant ritual of blood sacrifices. Ratification is the act of signing or giving formal consent to a treaty, contract or agreement, making it officially valid and only voided by death. In Luke, Jesus says, "This cup is the new testament or covenant [ratified] in my Blood, which is shed (poured out) for you" Luke 22:20, AMPC.

The Blood of Jesus Redeems

To be redeemed means to compensate for the faults or bad aspects of something, or to gain or regain possession of something in the exchange for payment. For the born-again believer the Bible makes it clear—to be redeemed means to be delivered from sin (Ephesians 1:7). We no longer work to be redeemed. Once we accept God as our Lord and Savior, the blood has made us Holy (1 Peter 1:13-23 and Galatians 3:13-14).

The Blood of Jesus Cleanses us and Makes us Righteous (in Right Standing with God)

Both Romans 3:21-25 and Revelation 1:5 shows that once you become born again, your old self dies, and your true self awakens. You are now filled with the Holy Spirit. You are a new creature in Christ (2 Corinthians 5:17). What this means is that your old life is gone. You do not have to keep dwelling on the mistakes (sin) of the past. God does not remember them so why should you? While Paul was still known as Saul, he was one of the biggest persecutors of believers (Acts 8:3), but God chose to use him as an "instrument to take my message to the Gentiles and to the kings, as well as to the people of Israel" (Acts 9:15, NLT). Once Paul became a Believer (Acts 9:18), his former acts were immediately forgotten. He (Paul) said, "I wronged no one" because he refused to be associated with the past of his old self (his "old" man). Once you choose to become a Christian, you become a new person. You are not the same anymore. This means that anyone who belongs to Christ has become a new person. The old life is gone. A new life has begun! You can say, "I have wronged no one!"

The Blood of Jesus Heals

The power to be healed was given to us through the blood of Jesus. In Isaiah it states, "He (Jesus) was wounded for our transgressions and bruised for our iniquities. The chastisement of our peace was upon Him and by His stripes we are healed" Isaiah 53:5, KJV. This scripture isn't talking about something that may happen. It is talking about what has already happened (we are healed). The lashes (the stripes) that Jesus took and the blood that He shed was for our healing.

The Blood of Jesus Gives us Power and Makes us Victorious

The power within the blood of Jesus has given us everything we need to live a victorious life right here on earth (Colossians 1:4-15). Satan already knows how powerful the blood of Jesus is "and they have overcome (conquered) him by means of the blood of the Lamb and by the utterance of their testimony" Revelation 12:11, AMP. How can you let something that is already defeated, defeat you? The answer is you can't! As believers, all we need to do is walk in our victory by trusting in God (1 John 5:4-6). Trust that God's promises will come true.

As a born-again Believer you no longer need to wait until you die and go to heaven to enjoy the things of God. He wants the best for you and wants you to experience the best right now while you are still in this world. He wants you to be whole; nothing missing, and nothing broken in every area of your life (your mind, body, and spirit). Through and by the blood your words have power. Because of the blood that Jesus shed, you have the same authority here on this earth as He *had* when He was here, and that He *has* while He is in heaven. You can speak to the mountain, whatever your mountain (obstacle) is, tell it to move, and it must obey (Mark 11:23). You can lay hands on the sick and they will recover (Mark 16:18). You can also cast out demons (any annoyance or hindrance) that tries to destroy your peace (Mark 16:17) and it must flee.

Is there anything the blood did not take care of?

Yes, the blood cannot take care of unbelief. As a believer, do not fall into the trap of choosing which parts of the Bible that you will believe. I am here to tell you to believe it *ALL!*

You must believe in and accept everything that Jesus sacrificed His blood for. If you don't believe that the blood ratified the New Covenant, then you choose to remain under the Law (the Old Covenant). If you don't believe that the blood has redeeming power, then you choose to believe that you are still a sinner versus knowing you are a Child of God who may have just missed the mark. If you do not believe the blood of Jesus cleanses then you choose to remain in the past, living with regret and unforgiveness. If you do not believe that the blood of Jesus has the power to heal then you choose to remain sick (1 Corinthians 11:39). And finally, if you do not believe that the blood has power and has given you authority and victory in this life, then you choose to remain mediocre.

Prayer

Father, I thank you for the blood that Jesus shed for me.
I thank you that it continues to ratify, redeem, cleanse, heal and give me victory.
I plead the blood over my family, and over all my relationships, past, present, and future, for only the blood can save, heal, deliver, and protect those who are near and dear to me.
I thank you for it all.
In Jesus' name
Amen

Dr. Wanda E. Hudson

Chapter 2

I am Saved now what
Moving forward based on the truth

"When we acknowledge that Christ is Lord and Savior over our lives, we are then born again. What is born again is our new spirit in Christ. Just by being born we had the old nature of Satan, now by being born again we have the new nature of Christ. We let go of the old and put on the new." Mintresa, 30ish

When asked about salvation (being born again) people generally mention that once you receive Christ as your Lord and Savior you will no longer go to hell when you die.

While that is true, it is only a fragment of what we will receive. Sure, God does not want anyone to go to hell (2 Peter 3:9) but being born again is so much more than that. In the book of John, it states, "For God so loved the world, that he gave his only begotten Son, that whosoever believeth in him should not perish but have everlasting life" John 3:16, KJV.

As a born-again Believer we have obtained an everlasting life. What does it mean to have an everlasting life?

If God gave it to us, it can't be a bad thing! Everlasting[3] is defined as lasting or enduring through all time, eternal, continuing for a long time or indefinitely. Our natural lives in this world, on the Earth, are temporal, but when we go home—our heavenly homes—our lives continue in heaven; we have an everlasting life.

3　　Everlasting (2019). In Merriam-Webster's Dictionary. Retrieved from Website

You also need to know that you have been saved once and for all time. As a born-again Believer, religion will have you believing that you are a sinner (saved by grace) every time you sin and that you have to do something to get back in "God's good graces." But when you are in a relationship with God and you read and study His Word for yourself, you will find out that is not true. In Isaiah 43:25, ESV, God says, "I, even I, am he who blots out your transgressions, for my sake, and remember your sins no more."

"To be born again is like a caterpillar evolving into a butterfly. You are essentially evolving into a better you." Jourdan, 24

Romans 10:9, NIV

If you declare with your mouth, "Jesus is Lord," and believe in your heart that God raised him from the dead, you will be saved.

Prayer for Salvation

Father God, I am sorry for my sins. Right now, I turn from sin and ask you to forgive me.

Thank you for sending Jesus to die on the cross for my sins.
Jesus, come into my heart as my Lord and Savior.
Thank you for forgiving me and giving me eternal life.
In Jesus' name
Amen

Renewing your Mind...it's a Process

"When you are born again, your life will be transformed for the worldly life you used to live. As you become more knowledgeable about the Word of God, you begin to have a desire to please the Lord and live for Him! Your old ways begin to change as you become transformed by the 'Renewing of your Mind.' As an educated woman, I was astonished in my Christian years at the information that I read in the Bible. I felt totally ignorant of the revelations that I discovered in God's Word. I only knew Bible stories from my years as a child in Sunday School. Today, my life is totally different from what it used to be! My thinking and mindset have matured because of the teachings, discovery and experimental relationship that I have with My Precious Lord and Savior. I know and Love the Father dearly. He has given me a marvelous life of Faith, hope, love, prosperity and expectation of a future with him!" Barbara, 79

To grow in the things of God you need to renew your mind: going from a carnal mindset (thinking that goes against the Word of God), to a spiritual mindset (thinking that lines up with the Word of God). In Romans 12:2, NLT, it states, "Don't copy the behavior and customs of this world, but let God transform you into a new person by changing the way you think. Then you will learn to know God's will for you, which is good and pleasing and perfect." God wants us to renew our mind to the many earthly blessings that we receive when we are born again. Keep in mind that renewing your mind is not a one-time thing, it is a process!

Have you ever started a new job and once you get there you decide to make some changes to existing policies and routines? Or, if you are an entrepreneur, you may tell your clients that you have decided to make a few changes to their accounts. Most likely the resistance will immediately come, followed by "but that is how we always do it." Once the changes are made, these same workers and clients, who were initially reluctant to change, are happier or even more profitable.

Renewing your mind is essentially getting rid of the "that is how I always do it" mentality. "People resist change because they believe they will lose something of value or fear they will not be able to adapt to the new thing."[4] These thoughts of loss and fear come before the thought of "this change may be better" even has the chance to form. We have to learn how to think the positive thoughts first; renew our mind.

Steps to take to renew our mind
- Ask the Holy Spirit for guidance
- Find a Church Home that teaches the Word
- Study, Study, Study

Ask the Holy Spirit for Guidance

Since you now know that renewing your mind is not a one-time task, that it is a process you will continue to do throughout your lifetime, the first thing you want to do is

---

4   Susanne Madse. Why is change so hard.Liquidplanner.com. January 11, 2018. https://www.liquidplanner.com/blog/why-is-organiza-tional-change-so-hard (accessed March 23, 2019)

allow the Holy Spirit to lead you through this journey.

Have you ever said to yourself, "Something told me that wasn't right"? That was not a Something, that was a SOMEONE! Once you allow the Holy Spirit to lead you, He will let you know when something is out of order. He speaks to us. When you have that feeling in the pit of your stomach or when the hair stands up on the back of your neck even when you have done the same thing time and time before, once you are born again, that's Him telling you to rethink this thing, renew your mind! He is speaking to you. Have a question? Just ask Him—He is your comforter; He will guide you into all good things.

Find a Church Home that Teaches the Word

Finding a church that teaches the Word of God is imperative to renewing the way you think. When you know God's Word, you will find that some of the words you have been using over your lifetime have either improved your life or stagnated it. I will be more specific on how to find your brook, your church home, in the section "Finding Your Brook and Your Authority in the Name of Jesus."

Study, Study, Study

A lot of the way we think comes from our culture and our environment; how we were raised and where we were raised. Our people group has a great influence on the way we think—we grew up thinking that a thing was either good or bad based on what our parents, grandparents and those

17

in our immediate surroundings may have thought. Unfortunately, that isn't always what God said. Renewing your mind involves reading and studying the Bible for yourself, to find out what God actually said.

When talking to other Believers about the Bible and the scriptures it contains, I often wondered how they knew things that I did not see in "my" Bible. This is where bibliology, the study of the Bible, comes into play. "Study to shew thyself approved" 2nd Timothy 2:15, KJV requires you to look beyond the 66 books in the Bible to get a complete understanding. Today there are several books to help you in the renewing-the-mind process. A few that I found helpful to have are: *The Bible Study Guide*, the *Companion Bible*, *The Bible Dictionary*, the *Bible Handbook* and the Bible Commentary. There is even a Bible for Dummies Series that is in plain language and very beneficial. With modern technology you can also search for additional information on your personal electronic gadgets. No matter how you choose to study remember that renewing the mind is a process and you determine how you proceed.

My mother, Barbara Carter, has gone home to be with the Lord but the first scripture I recall her reading was 1 Corinthians 13:11 ESV, "When I was a child I spoke as a child, I thought as a child, I reasoned as a child. When I became a man, I gave up childish ways." That was over 40 years ago, and I remember it as clear as if it was yesterday. As born-again Believers, that scripture fits us perfectly when it comes to renewing our minds. As a baby we learn to speak a certain way, to think a certain way and to come to certain conclusions based on what we were taught and by whom. Now, as our maturity as a Christian grows (when you become a man), the Word will challenge how you speak, how you think, and how you reason. Study to show thyself approved!

Prayer

Father, I thank you that my mind is constantly being renewed by your Word.
The way I used to think has changed based on the understanding I get from your Word.
Things that I used to say, I no longer say.
Things I previously agreed with I now know are not from you.
And things that I was taught that you said I now know were not from you but from man.
Thank you for allowing me to know you and your word for myself.
I am no longer a child, I am a man, therefore, I have put away childish things.
Your Word is true, and I am grateful for it.
Thank You
In Jesus' Name
Amen

The Bible - My Instructions for Spiritual Growth

"Being born again means you have decided to let Jesus guide you and you are a new creature in Christ, trying to do better than you did before. Making a conscious effort to be a better person." Anthea 52

As a born-again Believer you will want to read and understand the Bible for yourself, so that you can grow in the things of the Lord. 2 Timothy 2:15, KJV states, "Study to shew thyself approved unto God, a workman that needeth not to be ashamed, rightly dividing the word of truth." When reading this, my question was always, "What???? Approved by who?" Thinking that you need to be approved by a person can lead back to people bondage. Remember, as a born-again Believer, you have been set free from bondage.

To get a better understanding let's read 2 Timothy 2:15 in another translation of the Bible. In the Easy to Read Version the same scripture reads, "Do your best to be the kind of person God will accept and give yourself to him. Be a worker who has no reason to be ashamed of his work, one who applies the true teaching in the right way." Is that clearer? Does it give you a better understanding?

My point: do not let the wording in the King James translation of the Bible hinder you from knowing the Word. On Biblefacts.com[5] it states that there are hundreds of English translations of the Bible, 532 translations of the

---

5 Karin Lehnardt. 50 Amazing Bible Facts. Factretriever.com. August 3, 2017. https://factretriever.com/bible-facts. (accessed April 3, 2019)

entire Bible in a language other than English, and over 2,800 partial translations of the Bible in a language other than English. With all that Word available one should be just right for you.

Spiritual Growth

Growing in and understanding God's Word
will help you establish your prayer life
is for your edification
helps you determine the truth from a fact and
will strengthen your mind (your soul) so that you can accomplish His will for your life

What is Spiritual Growth?

When trying to find a definition for Spiritual Growth, I kept finding definitions like "growing to become more like Jesus," "growing to conform to be in Jesus' image," and "when the transformation process begins, spiritual growth starts." Thank God for the Holy Spirit! Now, you know as a born-again Believer, you are complete in Jesus as soon as you accept Him as your Lord and Savior (Colossians 2:8-10), and we were made in His image (Genesis 1:27).

Spiritual Growth isn't based on the number of scriptures you know, (even Satan knows the Word [Matthew 4:6]), the number of years you have been saved, or the amount of time you volunteer at the church. So, what exactly is Spiritual Growth? I'm glad you asked!

To me, Spiritual Growth is more of a verb than a noun; it is an action phrase versus being a thing. It is growing in the knowledge and things of God so that you can live a life of holiness and abundance. And before you get scared off, holiness is not long dresses, no makeup and church 24/7, 365. True holiness is just being dedicated to God.

Spiritual Growth is an advancing from infancy to maturity. Meaning not only being born again but also knowing the authority you now have as a Child of God, the authority you have by Jesus' name.

Spiritual Growth gives you wisdom to continue to stand on the Word, even when trials and tribulations come against you, challenging you, and ridiculing you for what you believe, (1 Corinthians 1:18-19).

Spiritual Growth also comes when you release old traditional ways of thinking and believing in order to renew your mind with the Word, (Romans 12:2), even when it is contrary to what you have "always done." When the Word has the final authority (the final say) over your life, you can say that you have truly grown.

Spiritual Growth will Help you Establish your Prayer Life

In Psalms, the people prayed for God's help like this: "Don't blame us for the sins of our parents. Hurry up and help us; we are at the end of our rope. You're famous for helping; God, give *us* a break. Your reputation is on the line. Pull us out of this mess, forgive us our sins do what you're famous for doing!" Psalm 79:8-9, MSG. This really does sound like a good prayer, and indeed it was good under the Old Covenant, but as you spiritually grow in the Word you will understand that you are under the New Covenant. The New Covenant tells you that God doesn't hold you guilty for your former sins nor does He forgive you for the sake of His name or to hold up His reputation. Twice in Hebrews (8:12 and 10:17), and again in Jeremiah 31:34, the Lord tells us that "our sins and iniquities He will remember no more." He repeats that again in Isaiah 43:25, and in verse 26 He takes it a little bit further by telling us to remind Him of what happened (refresh my memory about you). He wants us to tell Him what to remember about us.

In Isaiah 29:4, AMP, the Prophet Isaiah is telling the Israelites, "Then you (Jerusalem) will be brought low. You will speak from the earth, and from the dust where you lie face down your muffled voice will come. Your voice will also be like that of a spirit from earth [like one produced by a medium], and your speech will whisper and squeak from the dust." How can we be brought low as the dust? When you start reading the Word and using what it says as your guide for Spiritual Growth you know you will never be brought down as low as dust. As a born-again Believer you know you are one with Jesus and being created in His image is as high as one can get.

When you are growing spiritually in the Word you learn that prayer is not about going to God and pleading with Him to do something. You learn that everything you need you have the authority to command it to be. Prayer is just talking to God about the things that He already said you can have; what He has already provided for you. Your job is to be confident in the Word and to wait on its manifestation (made real, come into existence). Without Spiritual Growth a person would continue to be "hoping and wishing" instead of agreeing and resting in God's Word. The promises of God have already been made available to you. All that is left for you to do is Thank God and believe that you have already received what you have prayed for.

When you pray, take time to enjoy talking to God. Psalm 37:4, ESV, tells us to "Delight in the Lord and He will give you the desires of your heart." When it says delight in the Lord, it means to take time with Him. Serve Him. Enjoy His company and let Him enjoy you. He wants to commune with you, spend time with you. Don't only go to Him in time of despair; He is not your genie to answer your wishes, but He does answer prayers. Take time to thank Him for answering prayers even before you see it happen.

As a new Believer you may feel like you do not know how to pray. But you do: just speak God's Word back to Him. Tell Him what you want by using the promises that He has already made in His Word. For example, you can say, "Lord, my God, I cried to you for help and you healed me." This comes from Psalm 30:2, NASB; it's scripture that you used to pray for your healing. He promises it. You prayed for it, using His Words. Now thank Him for it! You are healed!

Spiritual Growth is for your Edification

Edification means improvement, instruction, or enlightenment, especially with moral or spiritual uplifting. It means to build up the soul. It is debris from the Latin word *aedificatione* which stands for construction, building, spiritual improvement. The Greek word for edification is *oikodome* which means mental improvement. In Philippians 1:6, AMPC, Paul says, "I am convinced *and* confident of this very thing, that He who has begun a good work in you will (continue to) perfect *and* complete it until the day of Christ Jesus (right up to the time of His return), developing (that good work) and perfecting and bringing it to full completion in you." Then in 2 Timothy 3:16-17, NLT, he says, "All Scripture is inspired by God and is useful to teach us what is true and to make us realize what is wrong in our lives. It corrects us when we are wrong and teaches us to do what is right. God uses it to prepare and equip his people to do every good work."

There is a saying that goes, "When you know better you do better." When you use the Bible as your instruction guide for Spiritual Growth, you know better. You have been edified!

With Spiritual Growth you will Know the Truth from a Fact

Let's say you have a doctor's visit and receive a bad report. Your doctor may say you have a sickness, then he/she adds, "The fact is this disease runs in your family. Un fortunately, there is not a cure, but I can put you on medication to control it." Or another example may be the fact that you have some sort of lack in your life right now and you may feel like you will never overcome it. As a born-again Believer, you are studying and growing spiritually in the Word. You have learned to believe what it says about you regardless of what people may say or what your current situation may dictate. You have learned The Truth! For sickness, the Truth is in Isaiah 53:5, KJV, and 1 Peter 2:24, KJV: "By His stripes we were healed." For lack, Paul wrote the Truth to his friends in Philippi when he was in jail. In Philippians 4:19, NLT, he stated to them, "And this same God who takes care of me will supply all your needs from his glorious riches, which have been given to us in Christ Jesus." A fact can change. Based on the situation, what was a fact yesterday may not be a fact today, But the Truth, it will remain the same. The Truth found in God's Word is the same yesterday, today, and forever.

Spiritual Growth will Give you the Strength to Accomplish God's Will for your Life

As a born-again Believer we learned that the Word would build us up so we will know God's Will for our life (to walk in our gift) and build the body of Christ. In The Message translation, Ephesians 4:11-13 tells us "Some of us have been given special ability as apostles; to others he has given the gift of being able to preach well; some have special ability in winning people to Christ, helping them to trust him as their Savior; still others have a gift for caring for God's people as a shepherd does his sheep, leading and teaching them in the ways of God. Why is it that he gives us these special abilities to do certain things best? It is that God's people will be equipped to do better work for him, building up the Church, the body of Christ, to a position of strength and maturity; until finally we all believe alike about our salvation and about our Savior, God's Son, and all become full-grown in the Lord—yes, to the point of being filled full with Christ."

How do you find your gift? Not in your strength, but in His. While attending World Changers Bible School to acquire my associate degree in Christian Studies, our "Blood of Jesus" class assignment was to witness to others and win ten souls for the Lord. I'm not sure how anyone else felt but I immediately dreaded the assignment. My first thought was, "I can't do this" or if I'm truly honest my actual thought was, "I don't want to do this." Why? Because I was depending on my own strength or lack thereof. I was allowing my feelings to get in the way of doing the thing God requires us to do (see I told you renewing the mind was a process). But the Word of God does not tell us to do things on our own. We are told to "Seek the Lord and His strength; yearn for and seek His face and to be in His presence continually" 1 Chronicles 16:11, AMPC. That is where our strength and knowledge come from; by seeking Him. Through His strength we can do all things (Philippians 4:9). And yes, I did complete the assignment and passed the class!

Once you are born again you automatically have the Trinity (God, Jesus and the Holy Spirit) inside of you. If you do not study the Word and grow in it, you may be able to hear the instructions they are giving you, but will you trust them? Will you believe in what you hear? Will you know enough to understand that your strength comes from the Lord and it is okay for you to act on what you hear?

When I was a child, I spake as a child, I understood as a child, I thought as a child: but when I became a man, I put away childish things 1st Corinthians 13:11, KJV.

That we henceforth be no more children, tossed to and fro, and carried about with every wind of doctrine, by the sleight of men, and cunning craftiness, whereby they lie in wait to deceive; But speaking the truth in love, may grow up into him in all things, which is the head, even Christ Ephesians 4:14-15, KJV.

Without Spiritual Growth, we remain as children. We walk around with a treasure map in our hand but do not open it so that it can lead us to the buried treasure. Your Bible is your treasure map. Open it! Read it! Study it! Allow it to help you grow into the person God has called you to be. Let it help you discover the treasures that are locked inside of you.

Prayer

Father, I thank you that I am growing in and by your
Word every day.
I thank you that your word has transforming power.
Your Word has helped me with my prayer life.

It has edified me.
It has shown me the truth and has given me strength,
and I thank you for it every day.
In Jesus' Name
Amen

Finding Your Brook - Your Church Home

"To be born again means, in the Christian faith, to be accepted by Jesus as you Lord and Savior as well as living your life to glorify Him." Tony, 32

Hebrew 10:25, KJV, states, "Not forsaking the assembling of ourselves together, as the manner of some is; but exhorting one another: and so much the more, as ye see the day approaching." With modern technology it is so easy and convenient to watch a church service online or on television, in the privacy of our own home. But the Word instructs us not to do that; it says, "not forsaking the assembling." These three words are what I want to touch on from this scripture: To "forsake" means to abandon, renounce or give up. To "assemble" means to gather together in one place for a common purpose. To "exhort" means to use a loud or enthusiastic urging any time you really want to encourage someone to do something. As a born-again Believer, how can you enthusiastically urge and encourage others to do something if you give up gathering in one place for a common purpose—the purpose of building your spiritual life?

Church Shopping versus Church Hopping

There is a difference between church shopping and church hopping. Google defines a church hopper as someone who desires not to settle at any particular local church, but would rather hop from church to church to suit their yearnings and/or, someone who finds themselves at a different church every couple of years for reasons beyond relocation, doctrine and philosophy of ministry[6].

I read an article in the blog Compelling Truth[7], and what it revealed to me is that people have different reason why they become church hoppers: (1) They have no intention of finding a permanent church home (no accountability to anyone); (2) They may criticize the preaching, the worship style, or a thousand of other things but the main issue, the problem, is their heart; (3) They want to continue the life-style they had before becoming a Believer; too much effort to live among a body of Believers; and (4) They feel the church doesn't meet their expectations, and it does not give them exactly what they want.

When looking for your church home—your brook—it is normal to visit several churches. As a Believer, your intention should be to find a permanent church home. When visiting a church, you want to listen to the teaching of the Man or Woman of God to ensure that it is sound and actually based on the Word. You also want to make sure there is a place for you to serve. This may take some time, but it will be well worth it to know you are at the place God intended you to be. The place where you can grow spiritually and learn His Will for your life.

---

6   Urbandictionary.com. February 17, 2015. https://www.urbandictionary.com. (accessed April 3, 2019)

7   Got Questions Ministry. Church Shopping. CompellingTruth. org. 2011-2019. https://www.compellingtruth.org/church-shopping.htmf. (accessed April 3, 2019)

When I Found My Church Home

When I met Roger, my husband, he told me that he went to World Changers (where the pastors are Creflo and Taffi Dollar). Because I had heard such negativity regarding this Pastor my first comment was, "Eel, don't ask me to go!" Well he didn't, but he did call me after Wednesday night Bible study, after he went to minister at the prisons on Friday night, and he would come over for breakfast after Sunday service. One particular Tuesday I said, "I'm going to church with you tomorrow," which would have been a Wednesday night Bible study. That Wednesday was a typical workday, but while I walked to my car to go home, then to church afterwards, this homeless man spat on me. Oh, I was so upset and felt so dirty. I immediately thought, "I can't hardly go anywhere now!" See, the devil tried to stop me from walking into my destiny. He didn't want me to find God's Will for my life. When I finally looked down at my outfit the spit had missed its mark and only landed on a bag I was carrying. Boy, was I relieved! I persevered and made my way to Bible study.

World Changers is described as a Megachurch, which is defined by Merriam-Webster's Dictionary[8] as a church having an extremely large congregation. The services are held in a building called the Dome. When I entered, Pastor Dollar was already ministering so I took my seat and started listening. Immediately it was like everything he was saying was directed towards me. In his natural comedic way, he

8   Megachurch (2019) In Merriam-Webster's Dictionary. Retrieved from Website.

was addressing all the negative things that I heard about the church. The other seats and the people in them seemed to disappear, I was the only one in the Dome. And when the Word came forth, he was not whooping and hollering or just reading scripture from the King James Bible. I not only understood the words he was reading from the Bible, I actually understood what he was talking about, so much that I wanted to go and read it for myself.

In July 2002 I officially became a member of World Changers Church International and have been a member ever since. It may not be the place for everybody, but I have found my brook. Finding your church home may not happen as quickly for you as it did for me but when you do find your place, as long as the Leader is ministering the Word and you have a place where you can spiritually grow and serve, you will be all right.

There is no set time limit for you to find your church home so don't rush the process. Instead, take your time, evaluate your options, and listen. God will tell you where He wants you to be.

Don't Forget to Pray

Remember, in a previous chapter I told you it is perfectly okay to use scripture as your prayer. As a Believer working on your prayer life, you can use this scripture to ask God to direct you to your brook. Just start with "Lord" then read Psalm 31:3, NIV, "Since you are my rock and my fortress, lead and guide me." Thank Him then listen for the answer. God already has a place for your Spiritual Growth, ask Him where He wants you, then devote yourself to that place.

Prayer

Father God, thank you that my church home has already been established.
Give me an ear to hear where You are sending me.
I know that I already have an assignment; so, Holy Spirit, lead me to the Man or Woman of God who has been given charge to watch over me.
Since you are my rock and my fortress lead and guide me
It's in Jesus Name that I thank you.
Amen

A Relationship with your Father

"To be born again simply means to acknowledge that you believe that Jesus Christ lived, died, and resurrected from the cross for our sins. Also, a renewed mindset of allowing God to enter your heart and not just your head."
Kaleff, 33

I heard a minister once say that he tells the born-again teens to start learning about God as He is in the New Testament—the loving God. Then he said, "A wrong understanding of God from the Old Testament leads to a misunderstanding of the nature of God in the New Testament."[9] Wow, I thought that was so profound!

In the Old Testament you have scriptures that tell stories that give you a misunderstanding of God's love: Lot's wife turning into salt (Genesis 19:26); the ground opening up and swallowing Dathan, Korah, Abiram, and their entire family with all their belongings (Numbers 16); not to mention the plagues that came over Egypt and all the curses that would come on those who did not follow the laws. While reading all this it is easy to make the decision that you could not have a relationship with a God who did such awful things. You received a wrong understanding of God's nature from the Old Testament.

The Old Testament was the time-period of the Law. Back when, if you did good, you got good; but if you did

---

9   Minister Michael Owens. Teen Ministry Leader. World Changers Church International Bible Study. January 23, 2019

35

bad, bad would come upon you. **But God!** Now, because of your relationship with God, through Jesus Christ, the Old Testament rules and punishments no longer apply to you.
God's Nature

When people say something is of God's "nature," what do they mean? Your nature can be defined as the properties, or attributes (a quality, character, or characteristic, ascribed to someone or something) by means of which something can be placed in its proper class or identified as being what it is[10]. Therefore, God's nature would be His character, the qualities used to identify Him as being who He is. In 1 John 4:7-8 KJV, it states, "Beloved, let us love one another; for love is of God; and every-one that loveth is born of God, and knoweth God. He that loveth not knoweth not God; for God is love." In the NLT, verse 7 says, "Love comes from God. God is Love!"

"The Son reflects the glory of God and shows exactly what God is like" Hebrews 1:3, NCV. "Exactly" is without discrepancy, precisely, adequately, in every aspect. Jesus is the very image of God's nature—He is the expression of God's love.

Genesis 1:26, KJV, In the beginning God said, "and let us make man in our image, in our likeness." John 14:6-11, NLT, Jesus told him, "I am the way, the truth, and the life. No one can come to the Father except through me. If you had really known me, you would know who my Father is. From now on, you do know him and have seen him!"

---

10   Nature (1996) Merriam-Webster's Dictionary

Philip said, "Lord, show us the Father, and we will be satisfied." Jesus replied, "Have I been with you all this time,

Philip, and yet you still don't know who I am? Anyone who has seen me has seen the Father! So why are you asking me to show him to you? Don't you believe that I am in the Father and the Father is in me? The words I speak are not my own, but my Father who lives in me does his work through me. Just believe that I am in the Father and the Father is in me. Or at least believe because of the work you have seen me do."

I share these verses of scripture to say this: Since God is Love and Love comes from God and you are made in His image, and Jesus, who is an expression of God's Love, is in you, then as a born-again Believer, when you stand in the mirror and look at yourself you will see that the greatest expression of God's Love is YOU! Your relationship with God is the manifestation (the finished product) of His Glory—His Nature!

Hebrews 3:5-6, KJV, discusses the relationship God had with Moses and Jesus. It states, "Moses was a faithful servant owned by God in God's house. He spoke of the things that would be told about later on. But Christ was faithful as a Son Who is Head of God's house. We are of God's house if we keep our trust in the Lord until the end. This is our hope." Through God's love you are no longer a servant of God but a son. Moses and those under the law were servants, But Jesus and those who are in Christ (that's you) are sons...that is RELATIONSHIP!

In the New Testament, Jesus has paid the price for our sins. Since you are now a part of the New Testament (the New Covenant) under Grace, you determine what your relationship with God is going to be. Whatever impression you have of God will determine how you receive from Him. Do you see Him as someone to be afraid of, as in the Old Testament? Or do you have a personal relationship with Him based on your understanding or His nature from the New Testament? It's your choice.

Prayer

Father, I know that the way to develop my relationship
with you is by studying your Word and by spending time
in your presence, communing with you.
Help me to keep the distractions of this world from hindering my time with you.
I make you my number one priority!
It is so. It is so. It is so.
In Jesus' Name
Amen

You already have a Helper

"The first act of sin wasn't eating from the forbidden tree; it was denying the help of the Holy Spirit to resist temptation." Michael O. Carter[11]

As humans we are Tri-part beings: we are a Spirit that has a Soul that lives in a Body. In Thessalonians 5:23, NLT, Paul told the Thessalonians, "may your whole spirit and soul and body be kept blameless until our Lord Jesus Christ comes again." When we accept Jesus as our Lord and Savior, our Spirit is instantly renewed (Ezekiel 36:26) and we become a new person in Christ (2nd Corinthians 5:17).

God gives the Holy Spirit (the Comforter) to the born-again Believer as an advocate. In John, Jesus tells the disciples, "And I will ask the Father, and he will give you another Advocate, who will never leave you. He is the Holy Spirit, who leads into all truth. The world cannot receive him, because it isn't looking for him and doesn't recognize him. But you know him, because he lives with you now and later will be in you" John 14:16-17, NLT. He, the Holy Spirit, will show you things to come and bring things to your remembrance if you allow Him (John 14:26).

The only requirement to receive the Holy Spirit is to be born again. The promise of the baptism in the Holy Spirit is for as many as have received Jesus Christ as their Savior (Acts 2:38-39).

---

11   Michael Orion Carter. Facebook. June 15, 2019. Used with permission.

Roles of the Holy Spirit

• He leads us

The Holy Spirit knows the course that we need to take to be equipped to accomplish our mission (Matthew 3:16 and 4:1).

• He Reveals the Truth

His presence within us empowers us so that we can understand and interpret God's Word. Jesus told His disciples, "When He, the Spirit of Truth, comes, He will guide you into all truth" John 16:13, NLT. He reveals the whole counsel of God as it relates to worship, doctrine, and Christian living. He is the ultimate guide, going before us and leading the way, removing all obstacles, guiding our understanding so that all things are made plain and clear. He leads us in the way we should go in all spiritual things, and even if we make an error, He is still able to lead us to the truth. He reveals that Jesus is who He said He is, and He gives glory to Christ in all things.

• He Reveals our Gifts

First Corinthians 12 describes the Spiritual Gifts given to Believers so that we can function as the body of Christ right here on earth. Many gifts (spirit of wisdom, message of knowledge, gift of faith, gift of healing, miraculous powers, gift of prophecy, discernment, speaking in tongues with interpretation) all given by the same Spirit; the Holy Spirit— our Comforter.

Finally, He empowers us to express the Fruit of the Spir

it in our lives. With Him dwelling in us we can show love, joy, peace, patience, kindness, goodness, faithfulness, gentleness, and self-control; emotions that we may not always

be able to express through our own self-efforts.

Thank God for this precious gift of the Holy Spirit and His work in our lives!

Prayer

Holy Spirit, you are welcome here.
Lead me. Guide me. Help me be still so that I can hear from you.
Tell me where you want me to go and what you want me to do.
It is by your lead that I will fulfill my purpose.
Thank you for developing your fruit within me.
When I want to get weary, you give me patience.
When I try to worry you are my peace.
When I try to be unforgiving you remind me that God has forgiven me.
Thank you for being my comforter, my advocate, my friend.
In Jesus' name
Amen

We are No Longer Under the Law, we are Under Grace

"To be born-again means to be free from the perfor-mance-based Laws of Moses and now having access to Grace and a relationship with Christ as Sons of God." Fonda, 55

In the New Living Translation, Hebrews, chapter 10, is entitled, *Christ's Sacrifice Once and for All.* In verses 1 through 18 it states, "The old system under the law of Moses was only a shadow, a dim preview of the good things to come, not the good things themselves. The sacrifices under that system were repeated again and again, year after year, but they were never able to provide perfect cleansing for those who came to worship. If they could have provided perfect cleansing, the sacrifices would have stopped, for the worshipers would have been purified once for all time, and their feelings of guilt would have disappeared. But instead, those sacrifices actually reminded them of their sins year after year. For it is not possible for the Blood of bulls and goats to take away sins. That is why, when Christ came into the world, he said to God, 'You did not want animal sacrifices or sin offerings. But you have given me a body to offer. You were not pleased with burnt offerings or other offerings for sin.' Then I said, 'Look, I have come to do your will, O God—as is written about me in the Scriptures.' First, Christ said, 'You did not want animal sacrifices or sin offerings or burnt offerings or other offerings for sin, nor were you pleased with them (though they are required by the law of Moses). Then he said, 'Look, I have come to do your will.' He cancels the first covenant in order to put the second into effect. For God's will was for us to be made holy by the sacrifice of the body of Jesus Christ, once for all time. Under the old covenant, the priest stands and ministers before the altar day after day, offering the same sacrifices again and again, which can never take away sins. But our High Priest offered himself to God as a single sacrifice for sins, good for all time. Then he sat down in the place of honor at God's right hand. There he waits until his enemies are humbled and made a footstool under his feet. For by that one offering he forever made perfect those who are being made holy. And the Holy Spirit also testifies that this is so. For he says, 'This is the new covenant I will make with my people on that day,' says the LORD: 'I will put my laws in their hearts, and I will write them on their minds.' Then he says, 'I will never again remember their sins and lawless deeds.' And when sins have been forgiven, there is no need to offer any more sacrifices. Amen!"

Under the Law there had to be yearly sacrifices so that the Israelites could be forgiven of their sins. When Jesus died on the cross, He settled things once and for all times. This means that Jesus took all our sin, and all of the judgement that was supposed to come onto man, up on the cross with Him, "If I be lifted up from the earth I will take all judgement unto me" John 12:31, KJV. We are no longer under the Law; we are under GRACE!

Law vs Grace in Action

The story of the birth of Abraham's two sons Ishmael and Isaac (Genesis 16, 18 and 21) can be compared to our relationship with God under the Old Covenant (the Law) and the New Covenant (Grace). One son was born out of self-effort; Sarah told Abraham to lay with her maid Hagar, producing Ishmael, while the other son was born based on the promise that God gave to Sarah that she would bear a son; Sarah at 90 years of age and Abraham at 100 years of age produced Isaac. God's Grace is Sufficient!

~~What~~ Who is Grace?

"Jesus is the Grace of God personified, and through Him, we are empowered to do and have things that we can't do or have in our own ability."[12]

Grace is not about what I must do for God to bless me; Grace is all about what He has done simply because He loves me.

Grace is not a curriculum, but we do study to show ourselves approved. In *Grace Rules*[13], a book by Steve McVey, he gives an explanation on what Jesus has provided for us through His death. It explains that Salvation is more than dying and going to heaven, having eternal life. It's also about having the same type of life down here on earth as we would in heaven. A Grace life. Unlike when we were under the Law, with Grace, we no longer have to rely on our own abilities to accomplish the things of God. With the Law it was all about our works, what we did to gain God's

12   Creflo A. Dollar. The Radical Life of Grace. (Creflo Dollar Ministries 2017) 125

13   Steve McVey. Grace Rules. (Harvest House Publishers 1998)

favor. With Grace it is all about what Jesus already did.

Grace Rules reminds us that the Law was given by God and had a reason for being created. It (the Law) was given to us so that we would know that we needed a Savior. As born-again Believers, not only did we receive salvation when Jesus died on the cross, we also received Grace, which is the unmerited, undeserved, unearned favor of God. We no longer live by the Law; we live by Grace. There is nothing that we can do to earn God's favor, no work that we could ever do for Him to love us more than He does at this exact moment.

Grace NOT a License to Sin

As Christians (Christ-like) we understand that there was NEVER a curse given in the New Testament for actions of disobedience or for missing the mark (sinning). Still, Grace does not give us a license to sin just because we know we are forgiven. On the contrary, "Grace will motivate a man to live a godly lifestyle more than a thousand laws could ever do."[14] With the freedom that Grace provides it will not cause a person to be inactive; Grace will push the Believer to be more active, to pursue a deeper relationship with God not because you have to, but because you get to. Grace can also allow a person to be more energized because it releases us from the servitude of religious duties.

Chapter 8 of *Grace Rules,* entitled "A Smiling God," breaks down any wrong thinking or preconceived notions

---

14   Steven McVey 91

that a person may have concerning God and who He is to us. When a student was asked to describe God, the answer reminded me of how I thought God was this detached being that only wanted to do for me if I was doing what was right, as long as I was serving Him. But as soon as I missed the mark, He would turn His back on me until I could do enough good to make up for the misconduct that I just did. With Grace, I now know once I chose Jesus as my Lord and Savior my relationship with God is irreversible. I am loved. I am forgiven. I am saved. I am blessed without ever having to worry about having the blessing taken away because I disappointed God! "Grace is a system of living whereby God blesses us because we are in Jesus Christ, and for no other reason at all."[15]

Prayer

Father, thank you for your Grace; it is sufficient.
I bind any traces of the Law that I may unknowingly cling to and release wisdom concerning your Grace to saturate my mind at this time.
Father, I thank you for being an all-knowing God.
It isn't about what I can do for You but about what You have already done for me.
I will never cease to thank you.
In Jesus' Name
Amen

---

15   Steven McVey 146

Chapter 3

The Blessings of God
His Promises are in His Word

"Being born again means another chance to do better, however, this time you're new and you're not alone. In the same way you trusted Him for salvation, trust Him for everything else! Welcome to your Betterment! In Jesus' Name!" Leonard, 60

Now that you know being born again means more than just not going to hell, it's time to start expecting and receiving your blessings, the blessings you were promised in the Word of God.

As a born-again Believer you have the same authority Jesus does to speak over things; you just have to trust and believe that you do. In Matthew 17:20, KJV, when the disciples asked Jesus why couldn't they cast out a spirit He told them, "Because of your unbelief: verily I say to you, if ye have faith as a grain of a mustard seed, ye shall say unto this mountain, remove hence to yonder place; and it shall remove; and nothing shall be impossible unto you."

When talking about the blessing I often hear people say, with great authority, "The blessing of the Lord makes me rich." Merriam-Webster's Dictionary defines rich as "having abundant possessions; especially material wealth, having high value or quality, magnificently impressive or vivid and deep in color"[16].

Do these definitions have the same meaning when we are talking about blessings from God? Did God just bless

---

16   Rich (1996) Merriam-Webster's Dictionary

us so that we could have material things? Abraham was blessed *and* he was very rich in livestock and in silver (Genesis 13:2). The Prodigal Son was rich, but he *was not* considered blessed until he lost everything and returned home (Luke 15:11-32). So what does it mean to be blessed?

The Blessing

Bless, Blessed, Blessing, and Blessings: these terms are mentioned in the Bible over 600 times. The first mention of being blessed is in Genesis 1:22. While God was still creating the world, it says He blessed them (all that He created).

When you are blessed, you are held in reverence or you are enjoying happiness; you are in a condition or state of being in God's grace or favor. God's intention and His desire to bless His people is a central focus of His covenant relationship with us.

The history of Israel begins with the promise of a blessing. The curse that came upon Adam after his disobedience to God was countered by God's promise to Abraham in Genesis 12:3, NIV, when He said, "All people of the earth will be blessed through you."

Riches and the Blessing

I once heard my pastor say something like, "You can have a million dollars but have bad health, then you are just a sick millionaire." What that means to me is having a lot of money doesn't make you rich if you are low in other aspects of your life. To be rich is much more than having a lot of money. Being rich money-wise is based on an individual's needs. One person may only need $100 to cover all their needs, while someone else may need millions to cover theirs. What determines if either one is rich? The blessing does!

We are Blessed

All Christians are blessed simply by believing in Christ, and by hearing and keeping His Word. In Luke 11:28 Jesus said, "More than that, blessed are those who hear the word of God and keep it!" Even though at times we may go through trials and tribulations, we are guaranteed to come out victorious. "Blessed is he whose transgression is forgiven, Whose sin is covered. Blessed is the man to whom the Lord does not impute iniquity, and in whose spirit is no deceit" Psalm 32:1-2, NKJV. "And if you are in Christ, then you are Abraham's seed, and heirs according to the promise" Galatians 3:29, NKJV. That is us! We are blessed!

So then why does Proverbs 10:22, NKJV, say, "The blessing of the Lord makes one rich," if being rich does not mean we are blessed. The entire scripture needs to be read in order to answer that question. The full scripture states, "The blessing of the Lord makes one rich and He adds no sorrow to it." In this context rich simply means prosperous (whole, nothing missing, nothing broken). God blesses us so that we are whole and without cares (sorrow).

When you are rich (materially), money is your source. Unfortunately, it can disappear in a moment, without notice (stock market crash, inflation, bad business, robbery) leaving you in lack. Riches also cannot get you into heaven. In Matthew 19:23-24, NKJV, Jesus tells the disciples, "Assuredly, I say to you that it is hard for a rich man to enter the kingdom of heaven. And again I say to you, it is easier for a camel to go through the eye of a needle than for a rich man to enter the kingdom of God." But the blessing will give you heaven right here on earth.

The Blessing is Power

"And you shall remember the Lord your God, for it is He who gives you power to get wealth, that He may establish His covenant which He swore to your fathers, as it is this day" Deuteronomy 8:18, NKJV.

The Blessing is Wisdom

"Joyful is the person who find wisdom, the one who gains understanding. For wisdom is more profitable than silver, and her wages are better than gold" Proverbs 3:13-14, NLT.

The Blessing is Patient and does not Seek Vengeance

"The Lord will help you defeat your enemies who come to fight against you. Your enemies will come against you one way, but they will run away from you seven different ways" Deuteronomy 28:7, ERV.

"Bless those who persecute you; bless and do not curse. Rejoice with those who rejoice, and weep with those who weep. Be of the same mind toward one another; do not be haughty in mind, but associate with the lowly. Do not be wise in your own estimation. Never repay evil for evil to anyone. Respect what is right in the sight of all people. If possible, so far as it depends on you, be at peace with all people. Never take your own revenge, beloved, but leave room for the wrath of God, for it is written: 'Vengeance is Mine, I will repay,' says the Lord. 'But if your enemy is hungry, feed him; if he is thirsty, give him a drink; for in so doing you will heap burning coals on his head. Do not be overcome by evil but overcome evil with good" Romans 13-21, NKJV.

Prosperity is the Blessing

"Beloved, I pray that you may prosper in all things and be in health, just as your soul prospers" 3 John 2, NKJV.

As a born-again Believer you know when we talk about prosperity we are not just talking about money; we mean that you are whole in every aspect of your life.

"Let them shout for joy and be glad Who favor my righteous cause; and let them say continually let the LORD be magnified, who has pleasure in the prosperity of His servant" Psalm 35:27, NKJV. God wants us to be prosperous not only in material things but in our spirits, bodies, and our soul.

"For you know the grace of our Lord Jesus Christ, that though He was rich, yet for your sakes He became poor, that you through His poverty might become rich" (2 Corinthians 8:9, NKJV.

Jesus became poor (broken, took on the sin nature) so that could be rich (whole and sin-free).

Prayer

Father God, thank you that I am blessed.
Your Word says the blessing makes me rich,
and I thank you for allowing me to know that rich does not mean just money.
There is nothing missing, and nothing broken in my life.
Father God, I thank you that I am blessed to be a blessing to others.
I am blessed going in and I am blessed going out.
Fill me up, God!
In Jesus's Name
Amen

Chapter 4

God Said
Your Authority in the Name of Jesus

"Being born again means being adopted into God's family." Lavonia, 60

In the very first chapter of the very first book of the Bible (our manual on how to live), God gave us authority in this world. "Then God said, 'Let us make mankind in our image, in our likeness, so that they may rule over the fish in the sea and the birds in the sky, over the livestock and all the wild animals, and over all the creatures that move along the ground' "So, God created mankind in his own image, in the image of God he created them; male and female he created them. God blessed them and said to them, 'Be fruitful and increase in number; fill the earth and subdue it. Rule over the fish in the sea and the birds in the sky and over every living creature that moves on the ground'" Genesis 1:26-28, NIV.

God has given you the authority to control your life by the words you speak. You just have to decide to speak against what you don't want and to claim what you do want. You control your destiny by the words you speak.

You have the right to speak with authority over:

1. Things that have come to harm you

When you hear of a major catastrophe do you ask yourself, "Why did God let that happen?" In the book of Mark, Jesus and the disciples are in a boat when the water and winds become threatening. Jesus was asleep in the front of the boat when the disciples woke Him up because they were afraid. "That day when evening came, he said to his disciples, 'Let us go over to the other side.' Leaving the crowd behind, they took him along, just as he was, in the boat. There were also other boats with him. A furious squall came up, and the waves broke over the boat, so that it was nearly swamped. Jesus was in the stern, sleeping on a cushion. The disciples woke him and said to him, 'Teacher, don't you care if we drown?' He got up, rebuked the wind and said to the waves, 'Quiet! Be still!' Then the wind died down and it was completely calm. He said to his disciples, 'Why are you so afraid? Do you still have no faith?' They were terrified and asked each other, 'Who is this? Even the wind and the waves obey him!'" Mark 4:35-41, NIV.

Who are you to proclaim no evil or harm will come upon you? If you are born again, you are in Christ, you have Him in you. The disciples are talking about you!

2. Sickness and disease

Like I mentioned in a previous chapter, if a doctor says you have (insert disease) because it runs in your family, speak, and believe the Word over the situation. Isaiah 53:5, KJV, states, "But he was wounded for our transgressions, he was bruised for our iniquities: the chastisement of our peace was upon him; and with his stripes we are healed." Or you can also confess Luke 10:19, NIV when Jesus said, "I have given you authority to trample on snakes and scorpions and to overcome all the power of the enemy; nothing will harm you."

You are healed, so open your mouth and claim it so that nothing in this world will harm you. Sickness may be too hard for the doctor, but nothing is too hard for God!

3. Over life and death

Often when a loved one dies, passes, or goes home to be with the Lord (so many different names to indicate that they have left this temporal world), the question is asked, "Why did God take my spouse/mother/child?" But in the Word Jesus tells us the exact opposite is true. He says, "The thief comes only to steal and kill and destroy; I have come that they may have life and have it to the full" John 10:10, NIV. Proverbs 18:21, ERV, also tells us, "The tongue can speak words that bring life and death. Those who love to talk must be ready to accept what it brings." And finally, in Psalm 91:14-16, CEV, The Lord says, "If you love me and truly know who I am, I will rescue you and keep you safe. When you are in trouble, call out to me. I will answer and be there to protect and honor you. You will live a long life and see my saving power." God is not the creator of death. Use the authority that He gave you and speak life over yourself and your loved ones.

Speaking to the Problem

In Mark, Jesus said, "For verily I say unto you, That whosoever shall say unto this mountain, Be thou removed, and be thou cast into the sea; and shall not doubt in his heart, but shall believe that those things which he saith shall come to pass; he shall have whatsoever he saith" Mark 11:23, KJV.

In his book, *Mountain Moving Faith*[17], Kenneth W. Hagin explains that there is a difference between speaking to your mountain and speaking about your mountain. He states, "When you put God's Word in your mouth, magnifying the Answer above all else, speaking to the mountain will cause it to move. Each time you begin to speak about the problem, remind yourself to speak to it, telling it to change and conform to what the Word says!"

Mr. Hagin also gives three steps that we can use to stop talking about the problem and start telling it to be moved:

1) Take a day and keep track of how many times you speak about the problem you're facing.
2) Go to God's Word—the Bible—and find out what it says about the problem.
3) Begin to replace your words about the situation with God's Word on the matter.

When things go wrong or do not go the way you planned or predicted, you need to stop blaming God, and the devil for that matter, and ask yourself, "Did I use my authority to control the situation or did I just let it happen?" As a child of God, you should no longer live by the rule of "Que sera sera, whatever will be will be," because God has given you

17   Kenneth Hagin. Mountain Moving Faith. (RHEMA Bible Church) 1993

the authority to use your words just like He did.

Paul explains the authority in God's Word when he tells how Abraham believed what God told him, even when his circumstances and sound thinking told him otherwise. "(As it is written, I have made thee a father of many nations,) before him whom he believed, even God, who quickeneth the dead, and calleth those things which be not as though they were" Romans 4:17, KJV. What does that mean? In the simplest terms it means stop saying the way it is and start saying the way it *will be* according to what God said.

The Message translation makes these verses clearer:
We call Abraham 'father' not because he got God's attention by living like a saint, but because God made something out of Abraham when he was a nobody. Isn't that what we've always read in Scripture, God saying to Abraham, 'I set you up as father of many peoples'? Abraham was first named 'father' and then became a father because he dared to trust God to do what only God could do: raise the dead to life, with a word make something out of nothing. When everything was hopeless, Abraham believed anyway, deciding to live not on the basis of what he saw he couldn't do but on what God said he would do. And so he was made father of a multitude of peoples.

Now you may say to yourself, "If I'm speaking something that plainly is not happening, isn't that lying?" I say no, it's having faith that the promises of God will come true. If you were telling a lie your intention would be to deceive people, and even yourself, into believing something that is not true. When you are speaking words that line up with the Word of God you are speaking by faith and not by what is going on around you. You are believing the Truth will happen.

When we use the authority that we have in Jesus' name, we not only change our surroundings, we can also change ourselves. We are released from people bondage when we speak forgiveness over our lives. We can receive deliverance of all health issues when we speak healing over our bodies. We can remove the burdens and disease of stress when we speak peace over our lives. We also usher in victory by what we declare over our lives.

Prayer

Father, thank you for the authority to use your Word to

change my circumstances.
You have given me the authority to speak over things that try to harm me.
I speak over sickness in my body, over life and death, and over my problems.
You gave me the authority to speak to my mountains, whatever my mountains, are and they will be removed.
There is no greater Word then your Word, Lord, and I thank you for allowing me to use it to have command over my life.
I am yours Lord – to do as You say!
In Jesus' Name
Amen

Chapter 5

Forgiveness
The Freedom to Just Let Go

"Being born again could be like forgiveness, a second chance or a fresh start. It could also be a cleansing of the soul." Anonymous, 32

Forgave, forgive, forgiven, forgiveness, forgives and forgiving. Six expressions of the same word. To forgive means to wipe the slate clean, to pardon, to cancel a debt. It also means you are giving up the right to hurt the person who has hurt you.

When forgiveness is mentioned you may think, "But wait…you don't know what he did to me." It really doesn't matter! Look what was done to Jesus and He immediately told God to forgive them. Luke 23:24, KJV, states, "Then said Jesus, 'Father forgive them; for they know not what they do.'"

When someone does something against you, yes, they should ask for your forgiveness but what happens when they don't? Do you hold on to your hurt and unforgiveness until they apologize or until you think they should be forgiven? No, because forgiveness is not for the other person; they might not even know, or care, that you are angry or hurt. Forgiveness is for you!

Reasons to Forgive:

Forgiveness is an act of obedience and submission to God's will.

In Matthew 6:14-15, AMP, Jesus said, "For if you

forgive others their trespasses [their reckless and willful sins], your heavenly Father will also forgive you. But if you do not forgive others, instead you nurture your hurt and anger until it interferes with your relationship with God, then your Father will not forgive your trespasses."

God doesn't want anything to interfere with your relationship with Him.

Forgiveness brings you peace.

"Never pay back evil for evil to anyone. Do things in such a way that everyone can see you are honorable. Do your part to live in peace with everyone" Romans 12:17-18, NLT.

How can you live in peace walking around the house not speaking to your spouse, children, or parents because of some slight that you feel was done against you? Do you part and squash it!

Forgiving is not forgetting; it's just about letting go of the hurt.

While in Rome Paul told the Believers, "Let all bitterness, and wrath, and anger and clamor and evil speaking be put away from you with all malice: and be ye kind to one another, tenderhearted, forgiving one another, even as God for Christ's sake hath forgiven you" Ephesians 4:31-32, KJV.

There is not an exception to this rule. Forgiveness must

be given no matter who the person is that betrays you.

Jesus knew Judas would betray Him don't you think He already knew your BFF (Best Friend Forever) would betray you? Still, we are instructed to "put away all" not some but ALL "anger, be kind and forgive."

We forgive so that we don't open a door that will allow Satan any entrance into our life."

The Lord said to Cain: "What's wrong with you? Why do you have such an angry look on your face? If you had done the right thing, you would be smiling. But you did the wrong thing, and now sin is waiting to attack you like a lion. Sin wants to destroy you, but don't you let it" Genesis 4:6-7, CEV. God was instructing Cain to have the right response: forgiveness, and not give a wrong response because if he did, he would open himself up to the attacks of the enemy. Well, Cain did not respond correctly and killed his brother Able based on a slight that he felt was done against him. His anger and unforgiveness resulted in God banishing him from his homeland, which took him out of the presence of God. Let your response be instant forgiveness—if it's not, it is wrong!

Forgiveness is for our Spiritual Growth

In Matthew 5:43-48, AMP, Jesus said, "You have heard that it was said, You shall love your neighbor (fellow man) and hate your enemy. But I say to you, love, [that is, unselfishly seek the best or higher good for your enemies] and pray for those who persecuted you, so that you may [show yourself to] be the children of your Father who is in

heaven; for He makes His sun rise on those who are evil and on

those who are good, and makes the rain fall on the righteous [those who are morally upright] and the unrighteous [the repentant, those who oppose Him]. For if you love [only] those who love you, what reward do you have? Do not even the tax collectors do that? And if you greet only your brothers [wishing them God's blessing and peace], what more [than others] are you doing? Do not even the Gentiles [who do not know the Lord] do that? You, therefore, will be perfect [growing into spiritual maturity both in mind and character, actively integrating godly values into your daily life], as your heavenly Father is perfect." That is the GROWTH that you are striving for!

How Many Times Must You Forgive?

You are commanded to forgive over and over again. "Then Peter came to Jesus and asked, 'Lord, how many times shall I forgive my brother or sister who sins against me? Up to seven times?' Peter thought he was being magnanimous. He asked if he should do what he thought was a great amount, thinking it was too much, and hoping Jesus would say, 'Oh, Peter, that is too much. Once is enough.' But Jesus answered, 'I tell you, not seven times, but seventy-seven times'" Matthew 18:21-22, NIV.

Again, in Luke 17:3-4, EHV, Jesus says, "Watch yourselves. If your brother sins, rebuke him. If he repents, forgive him. Even if he sins against you seven times in a day,

and seven times comes back to you and says, 'I repent', forgive him.'"

But forgiveness does not mean you continue to put up with the offense. My pastor often says, "Forgiveness is instant, restoration takes a while." You forgive a person so that you can move on and not stay in offense. But the trust that you had in the offender, THAT is what will have to be re-established if they value your relationship.

Remember this: forgiveness is not for the other person and it cannot be separated from love. If you chose to live with the Love of God being shown through you and having His love being the purpose of your life, then forgiving cannot be avoided. Forgiveness allows you to be free from stress and anxiety. It alleviates that tightness you feel when you see that person you are holding unforgiveness towards. Forgiveness is liberating!

Additionally, letting go of unforgiveness does not mean that now you and the offender will hold hands and sing "Kum-ba-ya," sit around and braid each other's hair, or even start hanging out again. What it means is that You are giving up the right to hurt them for hurting You. YOU ARE FREE!!

Mohandas Karamchand Gandhi (Mahatma Gandhi) was

an activist who was the leader of the Indian Independence movement against British Colonial Rule. Employing non

violent civil disobedience, he led India to independence and inspired movements for civil rights and freedom across the world. Gandhi once said, "The weak can never forgive;

forgiveness is the attribute of the strong"[18]. Be strong like Gandhi and forgive.

Prayer

The fruit of the spirit is forgiveness, for forgiveness is for my benefit.

Father I thank you that you are manifesting the will to forgive in me right now.

Thank you that my forgiveness is immediate and does not allow any gateway for Satan to enter my life.

In Colossians 3:13 Paul tells us that we must make allowances for each other's faults and forgive the person who offends us because You Father forgave us, now we must forgive others.

Holy Spirit set my will to immediately forgive no matter the offense.

In Jesus' Name

Amen

---

18   Mahatma Gandi. Wikipedia

Chapter 6

Your Peace
It's too valuable to lose

"Accepting the reality that my spiritual life has merit and I long to shout, sing, dance all over God's heaven once my physical body has been returned to the earth." Chris, 52

"Do not be anxious about anything, but in every situation, by prayer and petition, with thanksgiving, present your requests to God. And the peace of God, which transcends all understanding, will guard your hearts and your minds in Christ Jesus" Philippians 4:6-7, NIV.

Another scripture says, "You will keep in perfect peace those whose minds are steadfast, because they trust in you" Isaiah 26:3, NIV.

What is peace? Calmness? The existence of no fighting? Or is it more than that?

Spiritual Peace is described as: a deliberate state of psychological or spiritual calm despite the potential presence of stressors[19].

A Brother who serves in the Nursing Home Ministry with me at our church, Samuel Coleman, often says, "It's my choice to rejoice." You need to know that you determine your peace; it should not be dictated by your situation or circumstance. We all have negative things happen to us, just by being in this world, but it is your choice to rejoice. Why? Because the negativity in your life should not steal

---

19   Spiritual Peace. Merriam-Webster's Dictionary (1996)

your peace. There should not be any price that you pay for your peace—if it costs your peace, it is too expensive.

God did not tell us that everything would go according to our plans. On the contrary, Jesus said, "I have told you all this so that you may have peace in me. Here on earth you will have many trials and sorrows. But take heart, because I have overcome the world" John 16:33, NLT. Our peace does not come from our actions or what we can control. Our peace comes directly from Jesus. He has overcome the world!

Prayer

Peace be Still!
In Jesus' Name
Amen

Conclusion

To say it is too hard to be saved may not be the correct wording. Yes, it does require actions on our part, but God has provided us with everything we need to ensure acquire the blessings that come with being born again.

I am going to close with The Message translation of Matthew 11:28-30:

Jesus said, "Are you tired? Worn out? Burned out on religion? Come to me. Get away with me and you'll recover your life. I'll show you how to take a real rest. Walk with me and work with me—watch how I do it. Learn the unforced rhythms of grace. I won't lay anything heavy or ill-fitting on you. Keep company with me and you'll learn to live freely and lightly."

It is **not** too hard to be saved when you are in the company of the Lord!

Final Prayer

Father God, I come boldly before your throne thanking
you for what you have already done for me.
Father, I thank you that there is nothing missing or broken
in my life.
Father God you know the plans that you have for me
which are for my good and I thank you that I walk in the
authority that you have given me to succeed.
When I am feeling guilty of my past You remind me that
you are the one who remembers my sins no more, and that
you want me to tell you what to remember about me.

When I am feeling lonely, remind me that you are always
with me and will never leave or forsake me.
When I am feeling unloved bring to my remembrance that
you love me so much that you gave your only begotten
Son so that everyone who believes in you will not perish
but have eternal life.
And finally, Father God, I thank you for removing all
bitterness and unforgiveness from me right now.
These things are just a weapon of the enemy to hold me
down and I proclaim that no weapon formed against me
will prosper.
I thank you that I continue to grow and walk in your love
daily.
In Jesus' name
Amen!

Dr. Wanda E. Hudson

www.ingramcontent.com/pod-product-compliance
Lightning Source LLC
Chambersburg PA
CBHW060137050426

42448CB00010B/2167